INSTAGRAM
STORIES

The SECRET
to Make Passive Income Stream
with Instagram Marketing

PATRIC CHAN

Instagram Stories

The Secret to Make Passive Income Stream with Instagram Marketing

Patric Chan

Table of Contents

What are Instagram Stories: an introduction to stories

In the era of social sharing, knowing what stories are and how they are created on Instagram is essential . Instagram stories are a creative and fun way to share your everyday life on the web, using flair and creativity to create engaging and entertaining videos that can be very successful in terms of taking on the public.

The functionality of the stories is born on Snapchat, but very little later in August 2016 they are implemented on Instagram , where they grow rapidly in popularity until they are used today by about 250 million users every day. Coming back to ephemeral contents, they can be viewed for only 24 hours, showing moments of daily life, but also the most funny and creative aspects of one's personality. Even the brands have learned to use them to make their products known; celebrities use them to keep fans updated and to show a more human and less glossy face.

Essential notes to create a story on Instagram

To create a story on Instagram, you need to access the application and click on your own profile image inside the rod in the upper left corner of the main screen, or you need to swipe your finger to the right to directly activate the camera for recording the stories. You then need to hold the round button down to start recording. Removing the finger the video ends. Ready-made videos or images can also be loaded, by pressing the button at the bottom left or by scrolling up the screen with the camera ready to record, to access the archive.

Several options can be used to publish a story . That "Live" allows you to broadcast a video live on Instagram. In "Normal" mode , you can take 15 seconds of photos or videos. The "Boomerang" format allows you to play a three-second video in a loop, as if it were a

GIF. In "Without hold" mode , you can record a video without having to hold down the button, activating recording with a voice command. "Super zoom" allows you to create a video that enlarges the subject more and more as it is recorded. The "Rewind" mode allows you to publish a video played backwards. "Step One" is the Italian translation of the mode called in English "Stop-motion": this allows you to play in sequence a series of shots without interruptions, in order to create a video.

How to exploit the Stories in your online marketing plan?

By their nature, stories adapt well to two great communication strategies, which of course are not mutually exclusive, but simply start from different needs and tend towards equally different objectives.

1) Experimenting

Due to the fact that the Stories have a duration of 24 hours, they lend themselves well to being used to make tests and test ideas quickly, but above all with low consequences if the idea were unwelcome.

You can then test new colors, products, and why not also analyze the perception of your brand to evaluate a rebranding by taking advantage of the interactive survey function introduced last October.

These surveys are in fact a fun and alternative way to engage the public and get fast and direct feedback, both for you and your audience.

But be careful, the possibility of being able to experiment does not mean publishing "without any knowledge of the facts" "just to try".

As in all web marketing activities, the tests must also be the result of strategic planning, which includes an action plan, time planning, an analysis and evaluation phase.

How to develop a process of experimenting ideas

A process that takes inspiration from the method of validation of ideas in the startup world, and that you can easily use also to strategically follow and experiment your ideas with Instagram stories, basically consists of 4 phases:

- Brainstorming Idea. Develop the idea you want to test, the goal you want to achieve and also make a projection of the result you expect, or that can be decisive for considering the idea valid or to be discarded.

- Content Development and Publication. This is the phase in which there is the creation of history and publication on Instagram. Of course it is important to exploit all the tools available from the platform.
- Data analysis. This is one of the most important steps: analyze and read the metrics you have collected. On the analysis of the metrics you can read in the following paragraphs.
- Evaluation. Now is the time to take stock, or to assess whether your history has reached your expectations and objectives in terms of performance. And if the idea that you have experimented can be integrated into your communication activities or offer of products / services .

And then it all starts all over again with a new idea to develop.

2) Telling - Brand Storytelling

Whether you sell shoes, shirts or services, what is the real difference between you and your competitor?

Knowing how to tell and show the broad context in which your product is born and sold, which are precisely the everyday life of the company, the people who work there, and the idea that the brand manages to inspire. Or focus on Brand Storytelling .

Imagine your Instagram stories are a television program. Your goal in this case is to tell the brand in a way that is not possible through other channels, but above all to create a loyalty and expectation in your fans.

Do you remember when you were little and you knew perfectly well what time and channel your favorite cartoon was broadcast on? Think about whether you could achieve the same result with your Instagram channel.

It means creating and nurturing a community of loyalists who know you and appreciate you not only for your products but for the soul of your brand.

In addition to the stories there is more: the Live video!

Once you become familiar with Instagram Stories, and your audience is used to seeing your content, then you can feel safe and stream live with Instagram Live videos.

Precisely because it is a direct and you have no possibility of editing, improving the light, or canceling if the result is not satisfactory, it is important that everything is well planned.

The great advantage of going to Live is that your fans receive a notification as soon as you go on the air, reaching out to your audience in one fell swoop, for free. Furthermore, once the live broadcast is over, you can upload the video in the feed of your Story, so even those who failed to be present have 24 hours to watch the video again.

You can use Instagram Live to cover an event, a special moment, or an official announcement. Or even to interview a famous guest, or ask a question session.

Stories in evidence, what they are and how to use them

Here is one of the most significant new developments regarding Instagram Stories: the Stories in Evidence.

From now on you can create permanent stories, always visible on your profile, exactly under your bio and just before your feed.

Unlike the normal stories that disappear after 24 hours, these are contents specifically designed to be published and grouped together, which have the characteristic of lasting until you eliminate them yourself.

This new feature is extremely valuable for profiles, especially business ones, that want to easily offer and show certain content that they want users to see first.

The big brands, but not only, are already experimenting with the Stories in evidence. Everyone finding the strategy for their own goal, but above all using their imagination and experimenting with an alternative, but known way since it works in the creation and use of normal Stories, to express themselves, show the products and guide navigation by creating categories.

Here are some examples of usage.

The Instagram account decides to be consistent with the description in bio, or "discover and tell stories from the world" and use the featured stories to show original and surprising content generated by Instagram users around the world.

The famous Danish store of fashionable objects Tiger uses instead Stories Fixed to create product categories, almost as if it were an e-commerce.

BBC News in turn decides to use the highlighted strip to offer unpublished content that aims to involve users through a quiz about the events of the week, and to show the trend news.

How to check performance?

Whether you are using Instagram stories as a tool to experiment with some ideas, or as a channel to tell your brand and engage your fans, it is essential to measure the results achieved.

Reading and analyzing data on the performance of your Stories allows you to assess whether your strategy is working or not.

Even if you never get all the data you can get from sponsoring, there are some metrics that are definitely useful for evaluating the performance of your stories on Instagram.

Unique views

Indicate the number of people who have viewed your story, and it is directly related to the size of your followers, so it's a figure that reflects how your brand attracts your fans. But in addition to the number of people, Instagram insights let you see who, or which account, viewed your content.

Completion rate

If the History in its entirety is composed of several videos or photos, you will certainly have noticed that the first clip has more views than the last one.

Having the ability to see the exact number of views of each clip, you can safely calculate the drop-out rate from one content to another and evaluate what works best for your audience, and what least.

This metric is to be taken into account in the development of future strategies, thus choosing the right order of presentation, also creating hooks, advances, or call to action to encourage them to continue viewing until the last clip.

Public Report

Another useful fact to monitor is the percentage of your fans watching the stories.

According to the latest data collected, the average percentage of fans involved in the accounts of international brand accounts is around 3.7% of the total number of followers.

To calculate the average percentage of your fans who follow your stories over the course of a week, calculate the average number of users who have viewed your stories in a given week, and calculate the report on the total number of your followers.

And you could keep this metric as a goal to overcome in the coming weeks.

Replies to messages

Direct messages are a clear indication of your audience's involvement.

Especially if you have created a Call to Action, asking to comment or respond to a request, and receive many messages, it means that your story works well, and you did a good job!

10 Ways to increase engagement in 2019

According to research by Agorapulse, Instagram posts with at least one hashtag received 70% more likes and 392% more comments than those without hashtags.

With the decline in organic coverage and the increase in impressions paid with the algorithms introduced to push brands to pay for exposure, hashtags are still the best way to organically guide your social marketing campaigns, taking advantage of Instagram posts. to increase coverage on the platform.

Since you probably have the basics of Instagram hashtags, use this expert guide to learn advanced and intermediate Instagram hashtag strategies - including pro tips - to get in touch with your target audience.

The rate of involvement among Instagram customers is the highest in social media and strategically integrating these hashtags into your social strategy will help you improve your visibility and involvement . Let's see!

Instagram Hashtags Strategy #1: Focus Your Research

The research for hashtags before using them is important, since the more the hashtags are more relevant and targeted, the more you increase the chances of reaching a target audience that will interact with your published content.

Depending on your individual goals, there are many types of searches to find the best possible Instagram hashtags.

Here are the most effective techniques:

Search for relevant topics

A good starting point is the search for trends related to your business line (keywords that you currently use are a great place to start your hashtag search).

Inside the Instagram app, just tap the hourglass icon, then select "tag" from the drop-down menu and enter the hashtags in the Instagram search bar one at a time.

The results of each search will show all the main hashtags closely related to the searched hashtag, which will give you ideas for even more hashtags that you can use to reach and engage your audience.

Pro Tip:

Regularly scan the search results, then browse the posts that contain the Instagram hashtags to keep an eye on and note the hashtag trends that could be used in future posts.

Research your target audience

Instead of inserting general random hashtags at the end of your posts on Instagram, take a more targeted approach to growing your following trying to figure out what hashtags your audience is currently using and putting them in your posts (making sure you only use the hashtags that are relevant and contains the keywords that users interested in your type of business are actually looking for).

Remember to look over the number of results per hashtag and avoid abused ones .

Think in terms of specifications, because in general, the more the scope of a given hashtag is restricted, the more likely it is that users will be involved with the topics published with that hashtag.

Pro Tip:

For more focused engagement, analyze the long-tailed hashtags your audience is looking for.

For example, suppose you publish a photo of a site in Vancouver, Canada. Instead of running only hashtags
#Vancouver (about 18 million posts), you can also tag #VancouverBC (just over 900,000 posts) and, better yet, #VancouverBCCanada (less than 7,000 posts) to reach a wider

audience with less competition in the hashtag search.

Research executives in your field

One of the most effective ways to find the hashtags you should use is to Follow Instagram influencers and companies that share your target audience to see which hashtags they use. You'll probably discover some new hashtags to add to your arsenal.

Pro Tip:

Find the best brands in your space and ride their success directly in competition with them using the same Instagram-specific hashtag that they use.

More suggestions for finding potential Instagram hashsts

-   Perform a Google search on your hashtag without the "#" symbol - with and without spaces between words.

- Use a search tool like Hashtagify or Explore Ahrefs keywords to identify high performance hashtags.
- Search on Instagram, Twitter, Facebook and other social platforms to see if your hashtag has been used before.
- Make sure your hashtag doesn't have a second meaning that can confuse your potential audience.
- Check and double-check any acronyms you use in the hashtags for any potential double meaning.
- Perform your hashtags with another set of eyes by performing a pre-publication spell check to verify its accuracy.

Instagram Hashtags Strategy #2: The Art of Using Instagram Hashtag

There is a lot of research out there how many hashtags to use in each post to increase engagement.

Depending on the study you rely on, the best number of hashtags allows you to use intervals ranging from 5 to the maximum number allowed: 30.

Some marketing experts swear by the maximum use of hashtags with 30 in each post, but a TrackMaven analysis found that using 11 hashtags in each post is optimal to increase involvement on Instagram.

The reality is, the key to the success of the Instagram hashtag is to use them strategically, if you decide on three deeply sought after hashtags or on 30 carefully chosen.

Think of it this way. If your brand sells women's shoes, using a general hashtag like #WomensShoes will not help you stand out from the search results, which contain almost 193,000 other posts related to your specialty. But if you opt for another hashtag, for example #WomensFootwear, you will find that your post is one of only 20,000, which means that you are in a feed that has much less competition, increasing the chances of users finding your post.

Pro Tip:

Being as specific as possible with hashtags also limits the targeted consumer base, which makes it easier to build a busy audience .

Use special daily hashtags

Daily hashtags offer a way to interact with the public every day, keeping them constantly involved with content and connecting with them over the long term.

Instagram hashtag with the daily hashtag of the strategy

Here is a list of possible daily Instagram hashtags organized by day of the week:

- MON: #MondayBlues, #MondayVibes, #MondayMorning, #MotivationalMonday, #MondayMotivation, #MusicMonday
- TUE: #TuesdayVibes, #TuesdayTip, #TipTuesday, #TuesdayTreat, #TravelTuesday, #TuesdayTunes

- WED: #HumpDay, #WednesdayWisdom, WednesdayMotivation, Wednesday Wednesday, WednesdayWorkout
- THU: #ThrowbackTh Thursday, #TBT, #ThursdayThoughts, #ThursdayMorning, #ThursdayNight, #ThursdayMood
- FRI: #FridayNight, #FridayFeeling, FridayNightLights, #FlashBackFriday, #FridayFact, #FridayFun
- SAT: #SaturdayMorning, #SaturdayNight, #SelfieSaturday, #SaturdayLove, #SaturdayLunch
- SUN: #SundayFunday, #SundayMorning, #SundayBrunch, #SundaySpecial, #SundayMood

General rules of hashtag to keep things focused and simple

- Use a balanced combination of general, niche and location-based hashtags.
- Include a branded hashtag in every Instagram post.

- Use a campaign hashtag while running a marketing campaign or a gift.
- Think about using local holidays, events and hashtags to increase post visibility.

Instagram Hashtags Strategy # 3: how to hide hashtag

To keep readers focused on your well-written caption, it's a good idea to minimize the look of your Instagram hashtags, since the tags that stand out in posts often appear messy, spammy or out of place.

You can hide hashtags using one of the following two methods:

In captions

- After finishing the caption with a dot, press Enter (make sure you don't include a space after the last period).
- Enter a punctuation piece (a dot, a dash or a bullet), then press Enter again and repeat four times.
- Enter your hashtags after the last line.

- Hide Instagram hashtags after the example

It works because Instagram hides the subtitles after three lines, so your hashtags will not be visible unless your followers touch the "other" option or read the comments on your post.

In the comments

- Publish your content as usual, making sure to leave the hashtags out of the caption.
- Once you have posted your post, click on the balloon icon below to leave a comment.
- Enter your hashtags in the "Add a comment ..." box, then tap "Publish".
- After your post receives more comments, the hashtags will not be visible unless the user touches the "View all comments" button.

Instagram Hashtags Strategy # 4: Place hashtags in Instagram stories

Adding hashtag to Instagram Stories - in the text, in a sticker or in a position tag - gives your content another way to be found by a new audience.

But inserting hashtag in Instagram Story's images or videos doesn't guarantee this. Why? Because the hashtag aggregation depends on the quality of the published contents and their level of involvement.

Even so, with the ability to reach thousands of additional Instagrammers who might be interested in your brand, the Stories hashtag is definitely worth it.

In addition to using the same hashtags you use in standard posts, here are a couple of other ways to do it:

4a: use geographic tags

Research has shown that posts with marked positions get 79% more involvement than those without geographical tags.

When it comes to Instagram stories, location tags work almost the same way as conventional hashtags. There are only a couple of differences:
- Positions can only be published using stickers (text is not allowed) e
- Each photo or video can only have a position tag.

When you tag places like certain neighborhoods of a city, the tagged stories could reach local, state, regional and national audiences.

Pro Tip:

The location tag is an excellent way to promote local brick and mortar activities or increase exposure in a specific area , especially if Instagram inserts it into location-based stories in the exploration feed.

4b Use tags to expand your coverage

Creatively positioned, Instagram hashtags can be used as effective tools to grow your audience by engaging followers and touching their friends.

For example, a hairdresser sees that the hashtag #NYweddingplanners is trendy with their followers. While searching for related stories, the company discovers that most of the aggregated images are perfectly suited to brand positioning. So the show starts to publish stories with the hashtag #NYweddingplanners. When their images and videos are taken from the story of #NYweddingplanners, the designer begins to receive more click-throughs on their website through their link to the Instagram profile.

Pro Tip:

Follow the people who have already appreciated or followed your brand and take a look at the hashtags they use in their posts and stories, then use the same tags.

Instagram Hashtags Strategy 5: Use custom niche and hashtags

Instagram hashtags are available in many varieties and each has its own use and target audience.

Here's what you need to know about the main types of custom tags to define an effective strategy.

Niche hashtag

Niche hashtags are used to connect your brand to a specific target audience, the most likely to engage and do business with you. These special tags are particularly useful for small and medium-sized brands that hope to be seen in a wider sea of competition.

Pro Tip:

To find your weak point and reach a highly targeted audience, zero with very specific niche hashtags. If you look at vintage watch lovers, for example, the hashtag

#VintageWatches will place your post in a large feed with another 800,000. By using #VintageRolexWatch the search results are restricted to just 1,400 posts, offering a greater chance of exposure and conversions.

Brand Hashtag

These tags are unique to your brand on Instagram (or between social media platforms) and are a great way to raise awareness of your business and offer your followers a way to interact with you and each other.

Branded hashtags can be something as simple as the name of your company, the slogan or brand identity or it could also be related to specific products, services or marketing campaigns.

Pro Tip:

Try to make sure that your chosen brand is not already used by someone else.

Event hashtag

Event-specific hashtags (such as #BallDrop and #ArtBasel) are used to promote and guide participants, visitors and customers in real-world events, retail locations and local attractions, increasing engagement.

Pro Tip:

Make relevant hashtag event , descriptive, short and easy to understand. So make sure you use them before, during and after the event. Finally, don't forget to use the hashtags of events in offline promotions to drive traffic to your social media channels.

Instagram Hashtags Strategy #6: Use Argument from the hashtag channel

The topic channels, located at the top of the Explore section, represent a relatively new way in which users can browse different categories of published content.

Thematic channel channels vary based on the behavior of the users' platform and show the Instagram hashtags related to the channel displayed.

Because Instagram finds these hashtags important enough to be displayed, it's a safe bet that its members are using and searching for them.

Pro Tip:

Topic The hashtags of the channels are particularly useful for connecting with the still unnamed members of the target audience. So use the hashtags displayed in the topic channels in your posts to increase their profile and extend their reach.

Instagram Hashtags Strategy #7: Use hashtag to build communities

Find ways to use ultra-niche hashtag to target and interact with an active community or micro-community to increase the visibility and commitment of your brand by maintaining a conversation around your company.

The outdoor clothing retailer REI created a community and started a movement with #optoutside, which encouraged people to reconnect by exploring the great outdoors.

More than 11 million Instagram users shared their adventures using the hashtag.

Pro Tip:

To find community-oriented hashtags, do your research and see what Instagram hashtags your target audience uses when they talk about things about your brand, then adopt them. To create a community, offer users and consumers a reason to use the hashtag. (Whether it's a reward or sharing user-generated content, audiences respond best when they get something from the relationship.)

Instagram Hashtags Strategy #8: Add hashtag to your Instagram profile Bio

Since Instagram biographers only allow a standard hyperlink, adding hashtags to yours encourages people to start conversations and share experiences around your brand.

Instagram hashtags can now be inserted into profiles, a feature that provides the bios with an additional necessary punch by providing links to hashtag feeds.

Just don't expect to make your biography detectable in hashtag search results (it won't).

Pro Tip:

Enter "#" before each word in your profile and it will automatically become a clickable link that can be used for anything from the spotlight on branded content to promote the Instagram community you are creating.

Instagram Hashtags Strategy #9: Avoid forbidden hashtags

In an attempt to keep the content of the platform in line with its terms of use, Instagram prohibits - temporarily and permanently - certain hashtags, preventing them from appearing in search results.

While there is no complete list of forbidden Instagram hashtags, Instagram prohibits the violent, offensive, pornographic, illicit drug-related hashtag, focused on transactions, and the hate group, organized crime and terrorism.

But it also prohibits a list of apparently harmless ones!

For example, in the past, Instagram has banned some commonly used hashtags such as #curvygirl, #happythanksgiving and even #newyearsday due to excessive and improper use.

How to find out if the hashtags you use (or plan to use) are banned:

- Click on the magnifying glass icon to be displayed on the Explore page.
- Type the destination hashtag in the search bar.
- If the hashtag does not appear in the search results, it is prohibited (temporarily or permanently).

Note: forbidden hashtags can still appear in search results.

To confirm a call, touch the hashtag (if banned, it will link to a broken page).

Pro Tip:

If your posts receive fewer commitments (like and comment) or don't appear in searches, you could be under a shadowban . Being shadowbanned will prevent your Instagram posts from appearing to all users who don't follow you, which can hinder your growth. To avoid a shadowban, avoid illegal, risky and excessively controversial hashtags, and avoid exaggerating with tags and relying on hashtag tricks (using automated third-party apps to play the system).

Instagram Hashtags Strategy #10: Monitor hashtag performance

If you have an Instagram company profile (if you don't, that's why you should), you can see how effective your hashtags are and use the data to change your strategy to get more views and engagement.

Keep track of the hashtag performance of each of your posts will help you better focus your strategy.

To access this valuable feature, open any post, then tap the "View statistics" text below.

Then scroll up to see the full details of the post, including follow-up, coverage and impressions and how users found it.

Although Instagram Insights limits the time you can view the 7-day metrics for regular posts and 14 days for stories, there are some third-party apps that can provide deeper data.

Pro Tip:

It is important to continuously track, analyze, test and test which hashtags actually attract new followers and increase engagement.

What not to do with hashtag

- Don't use hashtags without doing research and managing them from your team for another perspective.
- Avoid using Instagram hashtags #ThatAreTooLongorComplicated, as it will be difficult for people to remember them.
- Never add hashtags after posting because tags added later are not displayed in searches.
- Stay away from all the lowercase hashtag phrases. Instead, capitalize the first letter of each word for readability.
- Don't expect people to use your branded hashtags without a reason or incentive.
- Never neglect to inform or educate your audience about what your hashtag means and how to use it.
- Don't think that the hashtags are enough! Respond quickly to all comments and engage your audience regularly.

The Instagram Hashtag cheatsheet

- Make sure that every hashtag you use is well thought out and relevant to your content.
- Avoid the use of generic hashtags, which will make you lose the post only in a generalized feed.
- Count hashtag because if you use more than 30, Instagram will block your post in searches.
- Manage your ideal audience and spy on the competition to find new and trendy hashtags.
- Follow your brand hashtag to stay updated on what people say about your brand.
- Keep track of industry hashtags to keep track of relevant news and trends.
- Keep all your hashtags organized in a spreadsheet where you can add metric data.

- Keep the most used hashtags in your smartphone's notes for quick and easy access.
- Create an Instagram hashtag strategy that includes different hashtags on all types of content.
- Have a plan to quickly remove or modify hashtag problems in case of problems or errors.

www.ingramcontent.com/pod-product-compliance
Lightning Source LLC
Chambersburg PA
CBHW051205170526
45158CB00005B/1822